Finding *the* Right Words *for* Life's Celebrations

Also by J. Beverly Daniel

FINDING THE RIGHT WORDS FOR THE HOLIDAYS

FINDING THE RIGHT WORDS

FINDING *the* RIGHT WORDS *for* LIFE'S CELEBRATIONS

PERFECT PHRASES FROM THE HEART

J. BEVERLY DANIEL

POCKET BOOKS

New York • London • Toronto • Sydney

POCKET BOOKS, a division of Simon & Schuster, Inc.
1230 Avenue of the Americas, New York, NY 10020

ISBN-13: 978-1-4165-3105-0
ISBN-10:   1-4165-3105-X

This Pocket Books hardcover edition April 2007

10   9   8   7   6   5   4   3   2   1

POCKET and colophon are registered trademarks of
Simon & Schuster, Inc.

Manufactured in the United States of America

For information regarding special discounts for bulk purchases,
please contact Simon & Schuster Special Sales at 1-800-456-6798
or business@simonandschuster.com.

To my granddaughter,
Molly,
who makes my life a daily celebration!

ACKNOWLEDGMENTS

Another book, another big thank you to my super family, John, Eric, Tracey, and George, and a special thank you to my granddaughter, Molly.

The many happy memories of past celebrations that I shared with my dad and mom, Frank Hoffman and the late Mildred Hoffman, will forever live in my heart. As will the joy and laughter I shared with my three brothers, John, Greg, and Joe when we were kids.

To my terrific editor, Micki Nuding, my heartfelt appreciation for all that she has done to make my books the success that they are today.

I have found my agent, Mary Tahan, of Mary M. Tahan Literary Agency, to be a real treasure. She has always been there for me and made my job much easier.

CONTENTS

HELPFUL HINTS FOR CREATING INVITATIONS AND ANNOUNCEMENTS 59

INTRODUCTION

Your best friend is having her first child and the baby shower is in two weeks. You've bought a card, but you'd like to write a personal note—something special, something memorable. After all, the guest of honor *is* your best friend. "With love" or "Sincerely" isn't enough, but your mind is blank. What do you do?

Never fear: *Finding the Right Words for Life's Celebrations* is here! It's the cure for your writer's block. In it you will find just the right thing to say for that baby shower, along with a whole treasury of phrases for many personal occasions, including christenings, Bar Mitzvahs, the birth of a baby, bridal showers, Thanksgiving, Valentine's Day, anniversary milestones—with a sublist of suggested gifts appropriate for each landmark anniversary—and much more.

National holidays, such as Grandparents Day, Administrative Professionals Day, Teacher Day, Boss Day, and St. Patrick's Day, among others, are also included in *Finding the Right Words for Life's Celebrations*. And at the back of the book you'll find a list of state abbreviations, and a holiday card recipient list.

The phrases in this handy little book will also jump-start your thought processes when you're called upon to give a toast. You'll find just the right words to fete Mom on her fiftieth birthday, or tell your brother how proud you are that he won the regional bowling trophy, or warm your daughter's heart on her wedding day.

Don't feel bound to use the phrases as written. Many are interchangeable and you can also combine two or three expressions. Have fun with them!

Simple and easy to use, *Finding the Right Words for Life's Celebrations* guarantees that you'll never be at a loss for words again.

Special Celebrations

CHRISTENING/BAPTISM

May your christening day be blessed with love and happiness
We are so joyful for you on your christening day
Wishing you much love as your life is now dedicated to God
May your christening be the beginning of a beautiful
    Christian life
The Lord now holds you in the cup of His tender hands

You were sent from heaven to celebrate this happy day and the rest of your life

The Lord is looking down and smiling at you on this glorious day

Wishing you much happiness now that the Lord has touched your life

Sending loving wishes on the holy baptism of your child

Welcome to your lifelong relationship with God

Being baptized is a true expression of your commitment to God

May God's loving hands guide you throughout your life

May peace and love surround you always

May the teachings of the Lord always be with you

Heavenly blessings as your baby is baptized

You are such a little bundle of energy. I hope the good Lord can keep up with you now that you are baptized!

May the angels watch over your precious baby today and forever

Wishing you much love and happiness as you embrace God and bring Him into your heart

May the good Lord guard and guide you always

May your heart be touched in a wonderful way on this special day

FIRST COMMUNION

*B*lessings to you as you feel God's grace in accepting Him
on your First Communion day

Can this sweet little angel be the same boy/girl that I last saw
wearing jeans and a T-shirt? Blessings on your First
Communion day.

May the Lord always bless you and keep you in His care

Sending you all good wishes as you receive the Body of
Christ for the first time

A lasting bond between you and the Lord has been formed
today

Wishing you a First Communion day full of love and joy

May your First Communion day be as special as you are

Sending many good wishes and the Lord's blessing on this
wonderful day

As you receive the Holy Eucharist on this day, may your
    heart be full of God's love

As you let Jesus into your heart, may He be a light to lead
    you into a life full of happiness and fulfillment

Many happy wishes wrapped in love are being sent your way
    on this happy day

Coming together with Christ on this glorious day is the
    beginning of many blessings

As you partake of the Bread of Life on your First
    Communion day, may your heart be full of joy and grace

As you let Jesus come into your heart on your First
    Communion day, may you forever rejoice in His love

Sending many happy wishes and prayers as you receive the
    Body of Christ for the first time

As you walk down the aisle with your head bowed and your
    hands held sweetly in prayer, rejoice

May the good Lord guard and protect you always

May the Lord lovingly hold you on this very special day

This brings loving prayers and special wishes for a
   wonderful First Communion
The Lord's blessings to you on your First Holy
   Communion day

CONFIRMATION

*M*ay God's love always be with you as you are confirmed
May the light of the Holy Spirit guide you throughout your life
On your confirmation day and always, may your faith and
    love grow stronger
As you are confirmed, may God's love be in your heart
Today is the day when you welcome the Holy Spirit into
    your heart
Many prayers and blessings are being sent your way on your
    confirmation day
May the Heavenly Father fill you with his love on this
    glorious day
Congratulations and many blessings on your confirmation day
May the power of prayer guide you forever
May the good Lord be your guiding light from this day forward

6   *J. Beverly Daniel*

Congratulations and many blessings as you are anointed with
the Holy Spirit

From this day forward may the Holy Spirit continue to bless
you with the gift of faith

The good Lord will give you courage, strength, and faith as
you are confirmed

May your confirmation day be a new beginning to a life of
faith and happiness

We wish you much joy as you walk hand in hand with the
Holy Spirit

There is no greater love than the love of God

May your confirmation day be a day filled with faith and
inspiration

Wishing you much love on this day as you accept the special
gift of the Holy Spirit

May the Holy Spirit surround you with His love

Your confirmation day is truly one of your spiritual life's
most precious moments

BAR MITZVAH

*M*ay the wisdom of the Torah help guide you through life

I know how hard you have worked to achieve this important goal in your life

May God bless you on this wonderful day when you become a young adult

How proud we are of you on this day of your Bar Mitzvah

Mazel tov at this time of your rite of passage

May your Bar Mitzvah be a wonderful turning point in your life

Your Bar Mitzvah has made you dedicated to learning and a son of the Commandments

May the traditions of the Bar Mitzvah be with you always

We know how much hard work has gone into the preparation for this day. God bless you.

Mazel tov on your Bar Mitzvah and your future

We are just as proud as your parents on your special day

Today you are a man and you bring honor to your family and friends

Where's it written that because today you become a young man, you can now stay out past midnight?

May your Bar Mitzvah inspire you to do great things throughout your life

As you start on this memorable new path in your life, may the wisdom of the Torah be with you

We have always been proud of you, but our pride is bursting on this wonderful occasion

This wonderful day will kick off a great year and a great life for you

It is a moment of great pride to be able to share in your day of accomplishment

May your years ahead be blessed with much joy and happiness

May you never cease striving for knowledge, happiness, and success

BAT MITZVAH

*W*ishing you much joy and many blessings on your Bat
  Mitzvah

Today, as you become a young woman, may the pride you
  feel be with you forever

Mazel tov on this happy day

May the teachings of the Torah be in your heart now and forever

You have always been a very special girl, but today you have
  become a very special young woman. Congratulations!

I know how hard you have worked toward this day. May God
  bless you.

Your Bat Mitzvah is the perfect day to set your goals for the future

May the wisdom of the Torah be there to guide you through life

It is a wondrous time when you become a daughter of the
  Commandments

Hoping that this rite of passage will bring you the joy you so
richly deserve

May the path you take in life be paved with the wisdom of
the Torah

Sending sincere good wishes and many congratulations on
this special day in your life

I feel honored to share this special occasion with a very
special friend

You have persevered in your dedication and we are so proud

We are here to celebrate the day when you are called to the Torah

Wishing you strength and guidance as you become a young
woman today

We will be thinking of you and your family with much pride
on your Bat Mitzvah

May you have a lifetime full of nothing but blue skies and
rainbows

You have always held a special place in my heart. Mazel tov.

May your Bat Mitzvah be a very precious occasion for you

BABY BOY

*M*ay the angels watch over your new baby boy

Baby boys mean baseballs, bats, and gloves! What a joy!

This precious little baby boy is a gift from God

May your baby boy's life be blessed with much love and
happiness

Be prepared for worms in pockets, scraped knees, and muddy
hands—the joys of having a boy!

Nothing can compare to the feeling you get the first time
your son hugs you and says, "I love you," for no reason

No shopping for frills and lace, it will be blue jeans and
T-shirts! Congratulations on your baby boy!

With you as parents, your son has a great beginning to a
wonderful life

I'll bet you're just glowing over the birth of your new baby boy!

You finally got it right and had a beautiful baby boy!

May you feel the love and warmth that the birth of a baby boy brings

Have you signed him up for Little League yet? Why wait?

A baby boy brings smiles, joy, and happiness. Congratulations!

May your son always have a special place in your heart

Your new baby boy will leave footprints on your hearts forever!

Your baby boy is a wonderful gift of love

Wishing you and your family much love and joy with the birth of your son

With the birth of your son, your family is now complete

May your baby boy be an eternal symbol of your special love

There is no love quite like the love between parent and child. Congratulations on the birth of your baby boy.

BABY GIRL

*T*here is nothing as meaningful as the day your daughter
    reaches up to take your hand

Sending many good wishes to your perfect little angel

Buttons, bows, and kissable toes—you're in for a lot of fun
    with your new baby girl

Your baby girl is a wonderful expression of God's love

I am tickled "pink" to be able to congratulate you on the birth
    of your beautiful baby girl

There has always been a special bond between a baby girl and
    her parents

Sending heartfelt good wishes and much love to your new
    baby girl

May your new baby girl bring love, laughter, and happiness
    to you and your family

May this wonderful pink bundle of joy bring much delight to you always

Wishing you much love and laughter with the birth of your beautiful daughter

Shopping for ruffles and lace is much more fun than shopping for jeans and T-shirts!

May you enjoy all the special delights of a baby girl

Your baby girl will steal your heart and hold it forever

May your new daughter light up your heart

May many blessings shower down upon your new baby girl

It is a very precious moment in life when you give birth to a baby girl

There is nothing as heartwarming as the little giggle that comes from a sweet baby girl

I'm certain your baby girl will have you wrapped around her little finger in a very short time!

There is nothing more joyous than the sweetness of a baby girl

There is an everlasting bond between parents and a baby girl

ADOPTION

$\mathcal{M}$ay your precious new angel live in your heart forever
With this new little treasure to love, your family is complete
How lucky your baby is to be chosen by you!
    Congratulations!
We are delighted to share in the joy of your adoption
    celebration
You have really been blessed by this wonderful addition to
    your family
All your dreams and wishes have finally come true.
    Congratulations!
Your beautiful adopted baby is truly a blessing from God
The child you have adopted has searched for the perfect
    parents and he/she has found them in you

Wishing you a lifetime of happiness and joy with your new
little one to love

You have overcome much and finally have the most precious
gift to love

Happiness to all, now that a new addition has joined your
family

With the adoption of your beautiful baby, a lasting bond has
now been formed

Wishing you many happy years ahead with your precious
new baby

By adopting this beautiful baby, you have given him/her an
anchor to his/her future. Congratulations.

Sending all good wishes to you and your family on the
miraculous arrival of your little one

You have finally found your pot of gold at the end of the
rainbow. Congratulations!

Thank you for including me in your special celebrations for
your new baby

You have waited so long for this happy day and now it is
    finally here. Sending much happiness to you.
We couldn't be more excited for you! Congratulations and
    best wishes always!
You have come to the end of a long search and finally found
    the perfect baby for you

BRIDAL SHOWER

*M*ay all the love you have come to know continue to grow

Another wonderful and joyous step toward your wedding day!

Sending showers of blessings for the bride-to-be

Wishing you every happiness on this most joyful day

Sending many wishes for a life full of love and laughter

There is a smile in my heart for the lovely bride-to-be

It's still not too late to back out! Oh well, congratulations anyway!

Because you are a very special bride-to-be, may you have a perfect day and a perfect future

Infinite blessings for your bridal shower and always

Today is the beginning of a lifetime of togetherness

May the sun shine brightly upon you today and always

You finally caught him! Happiness always!

May this wonderful day always have a special place in your heart

May this special day be the beginning of the pathway to a beautiful marriage

May your bridal shower be the start of a life full of loving, caring, and sharing

I've eaten your cooking. You had better keep the take-out restaurants on speed dial!

Sending many heartfelt happy wishes to you on this memorable day

Embrace this day and keep its happy memories close to your heart

Sending much love and happiness to the bride-to-be as we gather together for this happy occasion

Congratulations. You are not only the perfect couple, but also the best of friends.

BABY SHOWER

A new baby is one of God's most wondrous miracles.
Congratulations!

Sending all good wishes your way as the birth of your baby
gets closer

Get as much sleep as you can right now. There will only be
catnaps after the baby is here!

There is nothing more exciting than waiting for the arrival of
your new baby

The relationship between parent and child is the most
rewarding one

There is nothing as sweet as the scent of a baby. (Except
when they need a diaper change!)

The fun is only beginning now that your baby is on the way.
Happy days!

Babies are wonderful, but they should come with a book of
instructions

How happy and proud you must be as a new-mother-to-be

Your baby-to-be has picked the most wonderful parents-to-be

The birth of your new baby will simply light up your life

Now that your new baby is on its way, all your dreams will
finally come true

Sending many blessings to the happy mother-to-be

May your new baby be an eternal symbol of your love

May the angels always watch over your baby-to-be

You will find that cuddling with your baby will give you a
warm and fuzzy feeling of comfort

There is an everlasting bond between mother and child

With the birth of your new baby, your life will be full of
smiles, fun, and laughter

Sending much love and many hugs to you and your baby-to-be

With the birth of your new baby, you will be turning many
special moments into many happy memories

ANNIVERSARY MILESTONES

First Anniversary

May your first anniversary launch a lifetime of happy memories

I can't believe it's been a year and you're still on your honeymoon!

It's been 365 days since your wedding day, and they said it wouldn't last!

May your next fifty years be as happy as your first year

They say the first year is a "period of adjustment." Looks like you both came through with flying colors!

May all the joy and happiness you have felt through this first year multiply tenfold in the future

After one year love makes everything much sweeter

It's your paper anniversary, so I ordered a year's subscription to the newspaper for you

May this be the beginning of a lifetime full of love and happiness

As you celebrate your first anniversary, we wish you all the blessings for a wonderful future

Twenty-fifth Anniversary

God bless you on this twenty-fifth year of wedded bliss

Wishing you much happiness on your silver anniversary and always

Twenty-five years with the same person! Isn't it about time for a change?

Happy twenty-fifth and wishing you fifty more incredible years

May all your dreams come true on your silver anniversary and always

It's great to see the glow of love after twenty-five wonderful years

May your twenty-fifth anniversary be as special as you both are

How could you put up with each other for twenty-five years?
It must be love!

I would like to compliment you on twenty-five wonderful
years of marriage.

Sending many congratulations on the celebration of your
twenty-fifth anniversary

Fortieth Anniversary

You two look as great as you did on your wedding day forty
years ago

Being happy for forty years must have taken much love and
patience. Congratulations.

The secret to a happy marriage is a great sense of humor. You
both must have laughed a lot over forty years!

My compliments to two super people on forty years of
togetherness

Sending many happy wishes your way on the occasion of
your ruby anniversary

Please accept my heartiest congratulations on your fortieth
anniversary

May the magic of your love continue another forty years

May your fortieth anniversary be blessed by the angels above

Wishing you continued joy and happiness as you celebrate
your fortieth anniversary

I am in awe of the wonderful forty years you shared together

Fiftieth Anniversary

It must have taken the patience of a saint to survive fifty years
with the same person!

May your fiftieth anniversary be filled with special delights

May the celebration of your fiftieth anniversary light up your
hearts

In honor of your golden anniversary we send you all of our
good wishes

Fifty years! Who said it wouldn't last?!

You should have more spice in your life, so I'm sending you some oregano! Happy fiftieth anniversary!

May your fiftieth anniversary turn wonderful moments of celebration into many happy memories

Your wonderful fifty years of wedded bliss are an inspiration to us all

As you walk hand in hand on your fiftieth anniversary, may all your dreams come true

Sending much affection your way as you celebrate your fiftieth anniversary

Sixtieth Anniversary

Being married to the same person for sixty years is quite an accomplishment. Congratulations!

Sending much affection to two wonderful people on their diamond anniversary

May your sixtieth anniversary be a most memorable occasion

There were never two people more meant for each other than you two. Congratulations on your sixtieth anniversary.

Your love has flourished for sixty wonderful years

Love brought you together sixty years ago and warm companionship has made your life blissful

Love and laughter must be the basis for your wonderful life together

May the perfect couple have a perfect sixtieth anniversary

Your wonderful marriage has been an inspiration to us. Congratulations on your sixtieth anniversary.

We wish you much happiness and many congratulations on your sixtieth anniversary

ANNIVERSARY GIFT LIST

Anniversary	Traditional	Modern
First	paper	clocks
Second	cotton	china
Third	leather	crystal, glass
Fourth	books	electrical appliances
Fifth	wood	silverware
Sixth	sugar, candy	wood
Seventh	wool, copper	desk sets
Eighth	bronze, pottery	linens, laces
Ninth	pottery, willow	leather
Tenth	tin, aluminum	diamond jewelry
Eleventh	steel	fashion jewelry
Twelfth	silk, linen	pearls, colored gems
Thirteenth	lace	textiles, furs

Anniversary	Traditional	Modern
Fourteenth	ivory	gold jewelry
Fifteenth	crystal	watches
Twentieth	china	platinum
Twenty-fifth	silver	silver
Thirtieth	pearl	diamond
Thirty-fifth	coral	jade
Fortieth	ruby	ruby
Forty-fifth	sapphire	sapphire
Fiftieth	gold	gold
Fifty-fifth	emerald	emerald
Sixtieth	diamond	diamond

NEW JOB/PROMOTION

*Y*ou have worked so hard to achieve this goal. No one deserves it more than you.

Knowing you have done your best makes getting your promotion much sweeter

Congratulations on getting your great new job. We'll miss you, but can I have your desk?

It is quite an honor to be promoted to your new position. Congratulations.

Your new job will be quite a challenge, but I know you are up for it

Way to go! You got *my* promotion!

Your exceptional work ethic has made the road to your promotion a triumph

You have worked so hard through the years toward your promotion. Congratulations on reaching your goal.

"Get promotion" was #1 on your to-do list. Congratulations on completing your list.

I've watched you work and still wonder . . . how did you ever get this promotion?

Sending warm wishes of congratulations as you begin the journey to a brilliant future

I wish you all the best in your new position, but you will definitely be missed

We were so fortunate to have you with us, but we wish you all the best in your new position

Congratulations on getting your new job. Connections are always a big help!

May you inspire others to do as well as you have done. Congratulations.

You have accomplished much, but this is your crowning glory!

You have tackled and solved so many difficult problems, it's
    no wonder you got the promotion. Congratulations!
New job, new life, new stress! Good luck!
Way to go! Hip, hip, hooray! Congratulations!
Sincerest congratulations on your well-deserved promotion

GOOD-BYE/GOOD LUCK

Though we are happy about this great opportunity for you, we are also sad because you will be sorely missed

Wishing you much good luck and happiness in your new adventure

You will be missed. But may all your dreams come true.

May clear skies and smooth waters bring you safely to your destination

Your new venture sounds very exciting. Good-bye and good luck.

Wishing you all the best always. Can I have your office?

It is difficult to say good-bye, but it's the perfect time to set your goals for the future

Wishing you all happy days as you move on to greener pastures

Wishing you good luck as you begin your journey on the new
road you have chosen

Saying good-bye is difficult, but the memories we have will
last a lifetime

Though you're leaving, please remember to keep in touch

I will miss all our many laugh fests and coffee klatches!

Good-bye and good luck to the best friend a person could
have

Though it is hard to say good-bye, I couldn't be happier for you

As you leave us, please take along our heartfelt words of
thanks

You and your wonderful sense of humor will be deeply
missed

It saddens me to say good-bye to you, but I wish you much
love and good luck in your future

You have done a superb job and will be greatly missed

Sending you off with much good luck and pockets full of
shamrocks

Missing you already and you haven't even left yet

FIRST DAY OF SCHOOL

I can't believe you're starting school! Hip, hip, hooray for
   you!

Pre-K is the beginning of your learning adventure. Have fun!

Sending you hugs and kisses on your first day of kindergarten

Sending you off to your first day of school with much love

May you study hard, learn much, make new friends, and
   have a great first day at school

May your first day of kindergarten be a day to happily
   remember always

Summer is over and you're on your way to your first day of
   school. Have a great time!

Kindergarten is a wonderful beginning to your educational
   journey

May the sun shine brightly on your first day of school

How exciting your first day of school will be! Meeting new
friends, learning new things, and having fun.
Congratulations on your first day of school. You are growing
up so fast!
Wishing you a fun year ahead as you start school
Shopping for school supplies is the beginning of all the fun
you will have in school
I've known you since you were born, and I can't believe
you're starting school already
We are so happy to be sharing this special day with you
It's your first day of school and you are about to learn so
many wonderful things. Have fun, too!
We are wishing you all the best on your first day of school
We are so pleased to hear you are starting school.
Congratulations!
We are so proud of you as you start your first day of school
This is quite a milestone in your life. Have a great first day of
school.

GOING OFF TO COLLEGE

$\mathcal{W}$e're really going to miss you at home. Oops, gotta go, the decorators are here for our *new* den!

Happiness and good luck as you take a giant step toward a wonderful future

All your hard work has finally paid off and you're off to the magical world of college

Be studious, be good, and keep in touch by e-mail or letters!

We are delighted that you are off to college. Study hard and have a great time.

As you enter college, the possibilities are endless. Keep in mind, this is the beginning of a brilliant career.

I really admire the dedication you displayed on the journey to your education

Now you will really learn about life: cooking, cleaning, paying bills, and doing your own laundry!

Work hard to make all your dreams come true

Wishing you good luck in your college adventure

May your wisdom expand as you enter the world of higher learning

I know you can take care of yourself, but care packages for you are on my to-do list

You have always been an exceptional student and college will give you a wonderful opportunity to continue on this road

As you leave for college, I would like to leave you with these words of wisdom—study hard and behave yourself!

Treasure every moment as you enter the exciting world of a college education

May your transition to college life be an easy and happy experience

You are going to college to be educated, not to party! But I'm sure you'll do a little of both. Be good!

Going to college is a big milestone in life. Congratulations and good luck.

Please remember to clean your dorm room before we come to visit!

May your college education give you the opportunity to fulfill all your dreams for the future

BELATED WISHES

I'm really not late—just 360 days early for next year

Please accept my deep apologies for not being timely

I truly regret not being able to get this out on time

Forget you? Not me. Red-faced, that's me!

I am so embarrassed that the date completely slipped my mind

It was a terrible oversight on my part to have missed your birthday

I have no excuse for forgetting your birthday, but please forgive me

Though this greeting is late, it is well worth the wait

I truly apologize for my tardiness

To compensate for forgetting to get your card to you on time, I would like to treat you to lunch

I was so upset when I realized that I had forgotten your special day. Please forgive me.

Oops! Late again! Sorry!

I could say I had amnesia, but I don't think you would believe me

You know I have always been imperfect and that's why I'm late. Sorry.

We have so many happy moments to remember. I can't believe this one slipped my mind.

Though I am late, I hope your birthday was a happy one

Sorry I'm late. I wanted to send you an e-mail, but my cat ate my mouse.

Though your important day has passed, please accept my heartiest congratulations

If awards were given out for forgetfulness, I would probably be a winner!

I'm late. I'm an idiot! Please forgive me.

UNABLE TO ATTEND

I was so looking forward to your party, until I discovered
my husband had planned a surprise evening for me

My deepest regrets that I am unable to attend the gathering

Please forgive me, as I am unable to attend due to a previous
commitment

I was looking forward to attending until I realized that I had
made previous plans

Though I am not able to attend, let's make plans for an
evening out soon

Thank you so much for your kind invitation, but due to
previous plans we are forced to decline

It is with sadness and regret that I write to let you know that
we will be unable to attend

It is with sincere regret that we have to let you know that we
    unfortunately will not be able to attend

I am sincerely disappointed that we will be unable to attend
    one of your memorable evenings

Thank you so much for the lovely invitation, but due to
    unforeseen circumstances we are unable to attend

As you all gather together, please keep in mind that we wish
    we could be with you

Sending sincerest regrets for our inability to attend

It would have really brightened our day if we were able to
    attend, but unfortunately we have a previous commitment
    that we are required to honor

It was so thoughtful of you to invite us, but I'm sad to say we
    have plans that we are unable to break

Much to my regret, we are not able to attend

It really sounds like a fun-filled evening but we're sorry to
    say we won't be able to make it

I am so sorry that we will not be able to attend, and I
    apologize for any inconvenience this might cause

You'll never know how deeply we regret not being able to attend your party. You have always made your parties very special events.

I thank you so much for your gracious invitation, but I regret to say we are unable to attend

I am certain we are going to miss a most enjoyable evening, and I am so sorry to say that we are unable to attend

HOUSEWARMING

*S*ending you a bouquet of good wishes and much happiness
   as you begin your life in your new home
May peace and love abide with you in your new home
May the angels dwell within your home to guard and
   protect you
May your new home be filled with love and laughter
May the welcome mat always be found at your front door
God bless your happy home
Through the years, may you create many wonderful
   moments to remember in your home
Happy nesting!
Welcome to your new home. Keep in mind, the room with
   the stove and refrigerator is called the kitchen

May the only problems you have in your new home be little
    ones!

May you find the holidays extra fun as you decorate for each
    new season

Don't forget to put "snowblower" and "lawn mower" on
    your housewarming gift list!

Congratulations on moving on to greener pastures and
    finding the home of your dreams

Wishing you happy days and friendly neighbors in your new
    home

Happiness always to you and yours in your new home

With sincere wishes for all your dreams to come true in your
    new home

Kudos on finding the perfect home!

May many new memories begin in your new home

There is nothing as exciting as a new home in a new
    neighborhood. Congratulations.

A home is just a house if there's no laughter in it

RETIREMENT

*Y*ou now have no excuse not to clean out the garage!

Don't look at retirement as the end of something, when it is the beginning of newfound freedom

Congratulations on breaking free and starting on a new journey

Now you can live life in the fast lane! Congratulations!

What a great time to start building a new life

You're retiring? You mean you've been working?!

Have a great retirement and don't forget, it's never too late to take up skiing!

Wherever you go and whatever you do, may sunshine always follow you

Enjoy your retirement and make every day worthwhile

Pretend you're at work and sit back and relax

This is the time to spread your wings and fly!

Wishing you the best of everything today, tomorrow, and always

Retirement is just changing bosses

May your days be filled with love, peace, health, and happiness

We hate to see you leave, but your retirement is well deserved

Retirement is when you can finally be annoying all the time!

Wishing you much laughter and many smiles as you enjoy your retirement

You've started a new chapter in your life and you can really enjoy your morning coffee now

My prescription for a happy retirement: sunny days, peaceful nights, and much happiness

It's finally time for swaying palms, umbrella drinks, and a suntan!

ENGAGEMENT

*W*e are so happy that you have both found your hearts'
   desires
You played the mating game and the prize you won was each
   other
It is difficult to be perfect, but you two do it with such ease
May all the love you have come to know continue to grow
We have fallen under the spell of the great love you share
Sharing your life with someone you love makes the journey
   sweeter
It is so great to share this special day with special friends
May you both make beautiful music together forever
Your perfect love has been an inspiration to everyone
May the joy you share today grow deeper through the years
There is nothing like the magic of true love

Your engagement is the perfect pairing of two special people

Heart to heart and soul to soul, you were meant for each other

May this be the beginning of a lifetime full of love and happiness

Congratulations to you both as we celebrate the joy of your engagement

May God's blessing be yours forever

Wishing you much happiness as you celebrate a very special love

May your life together be all rainbows and no raindrops

May the angels watch over a perfect couple

May your love continue to grow with each passing year

WEDDING

*M*ay the circle of your rings be a reminder of love
everlasting

Sending you many good wishes wrapped in love on your
wedding day

As the wedding bells chime, may your hearts forever be
entwined

May all the dreams you are dreaming soon turn into dreams
come true

You always liked hanging out together, so you might as well
get married!

He chased you with so much enthusiasm, that you finally
caught him!

Wishing you a honeymoon full of magic and moonlight!

The honeymoon is short lived, so enjoy it while you can!

Our heartfelt wishes for a long and loving marriage

Congratulations on your sacred promise for the future

May this happy and precious moment be forever in your hearts

May you treasure today forever in your book of memories

May your marriage be blessed with an everlasting bond

I'm certain you both will be holding hands forever. (So neither of you can get to the credit cards!)

The sky's the limit for a wonderful future together

Wishing you companionship, contentment, and love

Cherish and love each other now and forever

Wishing you a wedding day full of all the love your hearts can hold

May this blessed union fill you with love, happiness, and laughter

The glue that holds two people together is love and a great sense of humor

GRADUATION

*D*iploma? I didn't even know you could spell the word!
  Way to go!

To graduate with high honors is a major achievement

May your graduation day always be a shining reminder of all
  that you have accomplished

I so admire the determination you displayed in achieving
  your goals

The reality is that now you'll have to go out and actually get a
  job!

Congratulations on your promotion to the _____ grade. I'm so
  proud of you!

The ability to learn takes a great deal of dedication and hard
  work. This, you have done.

I can't believe you finally made it. Must be a mistake!

Congratulations on breaking free! The best is yet to come!

We're so proud of the perseverance you showed in reaching
for the stars and getting them

No more party time at college. Now you have to adjust to the
real world. Congratulations!

You have worked so hard and deserve many congratulations
on your achievement

Your persistence and tireless devotion to a higher education
have finally come to fruition

Graduate? Any idiot can do that!

Wishing you much prosperity and happiness in your brilliant
future

Kudos to the graduate. I knew you could do it! Congratulations.

Now that you have graduated, the world is your oyster

Graduation is quite a milestone in your pursuit of a great career

Through the years you have always shown what a good
education can do

Why is it we're so anxious to graduate, but then later in life
we always remember our school years as the happiest!

DIVORCE

$\mathcal{Y}$our divorce is three steps forward after you've spent your whole married life one step backward!

Divorce is not the end of the world. It can be a beautiful beginning.

Now that you have finally broken free, it's time to really start living

It took a lot of courage, but you were right to leave him/her

Just think, you were happily married for two whole years! (Although you were actually married for twenty.)

Sorry to hear about your divorce. Just remember that family and friends are here for you.

When Cupid shot his arrow, I told you to duck!

Sometimes the only solution to an unhappy marriage is
  divorce

Now that you got rid of that drip, you can finally find the
  man of your dreams

You put your heart and soul into your marriage, and I'm so
  sorry to see it didn't work out

Welcome to the happy world of freedom!

They should make a do-it-yourself divorce kit. It would
  make life much easier!

Sending many blessings as you enter a life full of
  independence and happiness

Your newfound freedom will make you feel as though you
  were living in a bad dream before

There is no better way to say it: Congratulations!

Live, love, laugh, and be happy!

When your spirits are down, don't forget, I am only a phone
  call away

Now you have a chance to find your real Prince Charming!

We are all so proud of you now that you have gotten rid of
  the albatross around your neck!
Your heart might be broken today, but I guarantee it will
  mend sooner than you think

Helpful Hints for Creating Invitations and Announcements

With today's changing world there really aren't any set rules for doing things. This would also include the creating of invitations and announcements.

With single parents giving birth, married women keeping their maiden names, and couples getting married on a beach, things have definitely become more individualized. It's great to be able to "do your own thing." This also holds true for announcing these events, and these announcements range anywhere from traditional to trendy. It is your celebration. Make it memorable!

Creating these yourself can be great fun. Or if you feel you need help, there are many websites to choose from to assist you.

Most invitations still require the same basic information—name, occasion, day, date, time, place, RSVP date, and if it is a surprise party. This includes birthdays, baby showers, and bridal showers.

A good idea for birthday party invitations, whether for a child or adult, would be to include which birthday is being celebrated (fifth, twenty-ninth, sixtieth).

Baby shower invitations require the same general information as those for birthdays, except remember to include where the mother-to-be is registered and who is hosting the shower. Another thing that could be included is the sex of the baby-to-be, if known. If you don't want to be that obvious, you could hint at it by the color of the invitation. This makes gift-giving much easier.

Bridal shower invitations, again, contain the same basic information as those for baby showers. With these invitations you should also include the décor the couple intends to have, their color scheme, and where they are registered. Another cute idea is to include a small note that contains their mini–love story, along with a photo of the couple. As some of the guests will not know the groom, and some will not know the bride, it would be great to include where they are both from, where they met, when and how the proposal occurred, and when they became engaged.

Anniversary party invitations require the same basic information as the baby and bridal showers. A cute and clever idea for these is to include their photo and their mini–love story, also.

Engagement announcements may range from formal to unconventional. It's your engagement, and the announcements should reflect your personality. A photo of you and your fiancé would make a great addition. The information should include your and your fiancé's names, both sets of parents' names, and the date of the upcoming nuptials. A mini–love story would be a clever and unique addition to this announcement.

Wedding announcements usually are more formal, but again, it's your wedding. And let's face it, some weddings are *very* unconventional, taking place anywhere from a church to a hot air balloon to underwater. To help you choose the wording, printers have catalogs of samples, and there are also very helpful websites. Be sure to order more invitations than you think you will need, as sometimes the unexpected happens and you don't want to run short. The envelopes should be hand-addressed in ink and posted six to eight weeks before the wedding.

Birth announcements are very exciting to do because you can have so much fun with them! The perfect time to send them out is approximately one month after the birth. A photo is a very important part of the announcement. Necessary information would be: boy or girl; name; day, date and time of birth; and the parents' names. Height and weight are optional. There are so many clever ways of presenting the new baby. The announcement could be written through the eyes of siblings or from the family pet. It could also say, "Hello to our new little fireman," "hockey player," "ballerina," "drama queen," etc. Have fun and be creative!

Holidays

GRANDPARENTS DAY

Celebrated the first Sunday after Labor Day

Phrases

Any of the nicknames for grandparents may be substituted in these phrases, such as: Grandma/Grandpa, Grandmom/Grand-dad, Gammy/Gamps, Gamma/Gampa, Nana/Papa.

You have always made me feel as if I was your very own
    grandchild [for adoptive grandparents or step-
    grandparents]

Thank you, Grandma, for all your patience, love, and
    understanding

Thank you, Grandpa, for always being there when I needed
    you most

I am a much better person for having you both as my
    grandparents

A grandmom and granddad are people you can always count
    on to tell you the truth

Even distance can't weaken the strong feelings I have for you,
    Grandma and Grandpa

You have made my days full of fun, laughter, and love

Your house has always felt like home to me

If I could have picked my grandparents, I would have picked
    you

To a grandma who is a forever friend

With grandparents, there is a warmth that is seldom spoken

It takes someone special to be a grandparent, and you are special

I'm sending you hugs and kisses on this Grandparents Day

Thanks to the greatest grandparents for continuing to spoil me, even though I'm all grown up

Grandma, I will never forget your wonderful cookie jar and all the treasures inside

There is no other place as warm and cozy as your kitchen, Grandma

There is nothing as comforting as going to Grandma and Grandpa's for a cup of coffee and homemade cookies

I've packed my bags. I'm leaving home. I'm coming to your house!

I have always been grateful for the generosity of your time and love

There is nothing like Grandma's lap when you feel sad or have a boo-boo

My gran'ther's rule was safer 'n 'tis to crow:
Don't never prophesy—onless ye know.
                              —*James Russell Lowell*

We are shaped and fashioned by what (whom) we love.
                              —*Johann Wolfgang von Goethe*

VALENTINE'S DAY

Celebrated February 14

Phrases

My heart belongs to you on Valentine's Day and always

Wishing you much love on this Valentine's Day

Just like cashmere, you give me a warm, fuzzy feeling

Will you be mine on Valentine's Day and forever?

To celebrate Valentine's Day, let's light the candles, turn out
the lights, put on some mood music, and pour the wine

May this Valentine's Day be filled with love and laughter

Looking forward to sharing my Valentine's Day with my
sweetheart

Every time I see you, I fall in love all over again

Hoping this card warms your heart with many happy memories

I searched the whole world over and finally found you

It doesn't take a frilly valentine to say I love you

When Cupid shot his arrow, I told you not to bend over!

Please "bee" mine, because you are my "honey"

I have your name written on my heart

Valentine's Day is the perfect time to say how much you mean to me

No card can convey how deep my feelings are for you

I just wanted to let you know how happy you make me on Valentine's Day, and every day

I never believed in love at first sight until I met you

You make me feel as though we're still on our honeymoon

Let me make this crystal clear . . . I love you!

FAMOUS QUOTES

There be none of Beauty's daughters
With a magic like thee;
And like music on the waters
Is thy sweet voice to me.

—*Lord Byron*

All mankind love a lover.

—*Ralph Waldo Emerson*

ST. PATRICK'S DAY

Celebrated March 17

Phrases

May you find your pot of gold at the end of your rainbow

May the luck of the Irish be yours all year long

We're sending warm wishes for a happy St. Patrick's Day
across the miles to you and yours

Hope this message brightens your St. Patrick's Day

Hoping the luck o' the Irish finds you this glorious day

We're reaching out across the miles to say "Top o' the
Mornin'"

Sending an Irish smile to cheer you

It must have been the four-leaf clover I carry that sent you to me

We're wishing you happiness, joy, and good cheer on this
    St. Patrick's Day
May the leprechaun's magic touch you today
Happy "Wearin' o' the Green" today
Sending you wishes for love, luck, and laughter
May the luck of the Irish be with you today, tomorrow, and
    always
God's blessing on St. Patrick's Day and always
Irish friends are never far apart on St. Patrick's Day
I can smell the corned beef and cabbage already!
As you and your family gather for this wonderful St. Patrick's
    Day, I wish you much joy
With warmest regards for a super St. Patrick's Day
Everyone is Irish on St. Patrick's Day!
Wishing you a blessed and happy St. Patrick's Day

O Ireland, isn't it grand you look
Like a bride in her rich adornin'?
And with all the pent-up love of my heart
I bid you top o' the mornin'!

—John Locke

There is no language like the Irish for soothing and quieting.

—John Millington Synge

HALLOWEEN

Celebrated October 31

Phrases

Hoping your Halloween treat bag is as sweet as you

Ghosts, goblins, and things that go bump in the night. It's that time of year!

Scaring up the best wishes for a very happy Halloween

Wishing you a howling good Halloween

I'm sending chillingly good wishes for a happy Halloween

Best "witches" for a happy Halloween

Joining in the spirit of the holiday and wishing you a spooky Halloween

I'm completely spellbound by you

Light up the pumpkins. Boo! It's Halloween.

I'm batty over you

Hoping no black cats cross your path on Halloween

Wishing you a magical Halloween and a bag full of treats

Sending a magic spell to help fill your treat bag

May you get many treats on this spooky night

Happy pumpkin carving!

Hoping all the scary creatures are bashful tonight

May you have a delightfully scary Halloween

You have cast a spell on me and completely captured my heart

The witches are brewing up many treats for Halloween

Sending spookiest wishes for a great Halloween

'Tis now the very witching time of night,
When churchyards yawn and hell itself breathes out
Contagion to this world.

—William Shakespeare

Men say that in this midnight hour,
The disembodied have power
To wander as it liketh them,
By wizard oak and fairy stream.

—William Motherwell

THANKSGIVING

Celebrated the fourth Thursday of November

Phrases

We will be thinking of you as our hands encircle the table
   to give thanks

Thanksgiving is the opportunity to give thanks for all that we
   have

May your home abound with happiness and laughter as you
   share your Thanksgiving traditions with family and
   friends

All will be giving thanks, except poor Tom turkey!

We wish you a harvest of good wishes at Thanksgiving and
   always

Great holiday! Girls get to cook, guys get to watch football!
Hmmmm!

There is no other place I would rather be than home for
Thanksgiving

Sending prayers and lovely thoughts for this Thanksgiving Day

May the spirit of Thanksgiving be in our hearts all year long

Wishing you a joyous, healthy, and happy Thanksgiving

Sending a big hug on this wonderful Thanksgiving Day

You fill my heart with thankfulness on this special day

There is no time more fitting for giving thanks for all our
blessings than Thanksgiving

May you have a delicious and happy Thanksgiving

The anticipation is building as I think about all the
wonderful things Thanksgiving brings!

Sending wholehearted wishes for a very happy Thanksgiving

As you gather together during this wonderful holiday, I wish
you a blessed Thanksgiving

This happy Thanksgiving wish comes with much affection
and love

As you observe this wonderful holiday, my thoughts will be
    with you
Hoping your home is filled with an abundance of love and
    laughter during this wonderful holiday

FAMOUS QUOTES

I thank you for your voices, thank you,
Your most sweet voices.

— William Shakespeare

Come, ye thankful people, come,
Raise the song of harvest-home;
All is safely gathered in,
Ere the winter storms begin.

— Henry Alford

Professional Honorees

NATIONAL BOSS DAY

Celebrated October 16

Phrases

Thank you for making my job much easier by being an
   exceptional employer

I have always held you in high regard, and this special day
   gives me the opportunity to let you know

I would just like to make you aware of what a terrific job you
   are doing as a boss

You have always been a guiding light for all your employees

For all the years I have worked for you, you have made
coming to work a pleasure

Wishing a great Boss Day to a great boss!

Your care and concern for your employees has always been
appreciated

You have always set high standards for yourself, and it has
been a great example for all your employees to follow

Part of being a great boss is having consideration for your
employees. This you have done, and more.

There is no better way to say it: you are one super boss!

We would like you to know how highly you are thought of
by all your employees

As bosses go, you are outstanding!

Because of your deep concern for your employees, I look
forward to many more years of working for you

We would like to let you know that we hold you in the
highest esteem

Simply put, you are the finest boss a person could have

I would like to pay tribute to the world's greatest boss

It is such a pleasure to be working for the most thoughtful
boss a person could have

I feel very fortunate to have you as my employer

In honor of Boss Day, I would like you to know what a
pleasure it is to work for you

I would like to take this opportunity to say hip, hip, hooray to
a #1 boss!

FAMOUS QUOTES

Reason and judgment are the qualities of a leader.

—*Tacitus*

Success usually comes to those who are too busy to be
looking for it.

—*Henry David Thoreau*

NATIONAL NURSES DAY

Celebrated May 6
Week: May 6–May 12

Phrases

Your kindness and caring have made you an exceptional nurse

Your care and concern were so important to my complete recovery

I just wanted you to know that you have touched so many lives with your knowledge and skill

The nursing profession is so fortunate to have you as a wonderful example of what a nurse should be

I would like to commend you on your wonderful contributions to our community

Congratulations on Nurses Day for a job well done

It is difficult to be perfect, but to me you are the perfect nurse

Sending warmest wishes to a great nurse, on Nurses Day and
always

Nursing is a special gift that you use so caringly

Nurses are the backbone of the medical profession

One of the ways that you can tell you have a great nurse is
when she warms the bedpan!

Nursing is the toughest job you'll ever love

Nursing is a very difficult job, but you make it look so
effortless

Your wonderful spirit has put sunshine in my days

Thank you so much for your tender loving care

Your smiles and laughter have always helped your patients
make a speedy recovery

You are a great nurse and definitely have the healing touch

Your patients have been blessed to have a nurse as caring as you

I never believed a hospital stay could be pleasant until you
became my nurse

Happiness and moral duty are inseparably connected.

—*George Washington*

We are what we repeatedly do. Excellence, then, is not an act, but a habit.

—*Aristotle*

ADMINISTRATIVE PROFESSIONALS (SECRETARIES) DAY

Celebrated Wednesday of the last full week of April
Week: Last full week of April

Phrases

I would like you to know how grateful I am for all the
extra things you do at the office

With deep appreciation for all you do

Though I seldom show it, I am so grateful for your
dedication

May this little gift remind you of how much you are
appreciated

This office would never run as smoothly if not for you

The contributions you have made to this office have been
outstanding

Though your job can be very stressful, your professionalism
always shines through

You have a knack for accomplishing the impossible

Words say so little, when you have done so much

Thank you for your strength and support in chaotic times

A simple "thank you" is so inadequate for all you do

Thank you for going out of your way to get the job done

You have always made the impossible seem simple

Hoping the best things in life will always be yours

Thank you for your efficiency in keeping me so well
organized

You are extremely conscientious and your work ethic is
exceptional

Though you have faced many difficult tasks, you have always
seemed to accomplish them effortlessly

It means so much to be able to count on your dependability

Your loyalty and dedication to the job have always been
    exemplary
Your thoughtful ways have created a great rapport with
    customers

FAMOUS QUOTES

Fortitude is the marshal of thought, the armor of the will,
and the fort of reason.

—Francis Bacon

Duty is the most sublime word in our language. Do your
duty in all things. You cannot do more. You should never
wish to do less.

—General Robert E. Lee

NATIONAL TEACHER DAY

Celebrated Tuesday of the first full week of May

Phrases

You gave me a wonderful beginning, and I would like to
   acknowledge that meaningful gift

I have been so fortunate to have you as my teacher

Thank you for being a teacher I can depend on when I
   become perplexed

My teacher, my hero

Teaching is a wonderful profession, and you have been an
   exemplary teacher

You have been an inspiration to me to always do my best

You have always made the learning experience full of fun and
   laughter

How did you ever put up with me for all those years? But
 you did, and I thank you for it.

Sending many warm wishes to a very special teacher on
 National Teacher Day

Your dedication to the profession of teaching is outstanding

I would like to compliment you on the wonderful example
 you set for me and your many students

You have always inspired me to do the best I can. Thank you
 for your confidence.

The happy memories I have of my school years are due to
 your exceptional teaching methods

You have never failed to encourage your students to reach for
 the stars

Though you always worked so hard, you made it look so
 effortless

As I reflect upon my education, you will always be a very
 important part of my success

You are the world's greatest teacher!

A teacher touches a life forever

As we observe this wonderful celebration, I would like to
   send you all my best wishes
I would like to pay tribute to my favorite teacher on this
   special day

FAMOUS QUOTES

A teacher affects eternity; he can never tell where his
influence stops.

— *Henry Brooks Adams*

A teacher who can arouse a feeling for one single good
action, for one single good poem, accomplishes more than
he who fills our memory with rows on rows of natural
objects, classified with name and form.

— *Johann Wolfgang von Goethe*

PHYSICIANS

$\mathcal{Y}$our care and concern has made my healing progress quickly

Why does that tongue depressor taste like an orange popsicle?

There is nothing as difficult as finding the right physician,
and I am so glad I found you

When I called you for your opinion, I would have sworn I
heard someone in the background yelling, "Fore!"

The comfort and care you have shown our family has been
greatly appreciated

Stress is not going to the doctor, it's waiting for the bill
afterward

Your knowledge and skill have touched so many lives

Thank you for your sense of humor; it makes everything easier

I want to thank you for being so clear in your health care
information

You have always been there for us, whether it's been a cold or a medical emergency. Thank you.

The quality of service from you and your staff is continually excellent

You have been so supportive in my hour of need

Thank you for listening and caring

You have had a tremendous positive impact on all your patients

Your patients have truly been blessed to have a doctor as caring as you are

My health has greatly improved since I have been under your care

Thank you for helping me make informed decisions about my health care

We are so grateful that you are not only a great doctor, but also so kind and caring

We greatly appreciate that you answer our questions with easy-to-understand responses

We couldn't have chosen a better doctor!

The doctor sees all the weakness of mankind,
the lawyer all the wickedness, the theologian all
the stupidity.

— Arthur Schopenhauer

No physician, insofar as he is a physician, considers his
own good in what he prescribes, but the good of his
patient: for the true physician is also a ruler having the
human body as a subject, and is not a mere moneymaker.

— Plato

ATTORNEYS

*T*hank you for fighting so hard to help me achieve justice

I searched for the perfect attorney and finally found one in you

A fair attorney is the best friend you can have

When we needed the services of a lawyer, we were so fortunate to discover you

Your support and kindness have seen us through some very difficult times

Your wisdom has helped us make some very troublesome decisions

Your kindness and generosity have made you a superb attorney

What a great lawyer you are! But is that an ambulance siren I hear in the background?

We attribute your superior qualities to your being an
    extremely ethical attorney
Thank you for always being there for us
We consider you not only our legal adviser, but also our friend
We have always admired your ethics
It is difficult to be consummate, but you do it with dignity
    and ease
We so admire your ability to attain the best possible outcome
    for your clients
Your enthusiasm for justice has made you the great lawyer
    that you are
Through the years, it has been a pleasure to work with you as
    our attorney
It has been so comforting to be able to rely on you
Though I don't say it often enough, thank you for a job well
    done
You are a one-in-a-million attorney
I would like to commend you on your outstanding ability to
    accomplish the impossible

The leading rule for the lawyer, as for the man
of every other calling, is diligence.
Leave nothing for to-morrow
which can be done to-day.

—*Abraham Lincoln*

The good lawyer is not the man who has an eye to every
side and angle of contingency, and qualifies
all his qualifications, but who throws himself
on your part so heartily, that he can get you out of a scrape.

—*Ralph Waldo Emerson*

CLERGY

The kindness you have shown our family has truly been a
   gift from God

Through you, I feel God's presence daily

Your patience and understanding have shown me the path to
   greater happiness

I had never known such tranquillity until you joined our
   congregation

Thank you for making our parish come to life

May many blessings shower upon you and your near and
   dear ones

Wishing you much happiness and joy on this most special day

Hoping we touch your heart with our very special wishes

Your wonderful sense of humor has brought you closer to
   our hearts

God's blessings on you always

Through you, His light will always guide us

We count our many blessings because you have always been a
very caring pastor

We thank the Lord daily for your presence

Thank you for showing us the path to inner peace

Your guidance has shown us how to appreciate God's
wondrous ways

Your tireless devotion is always deeply appreciated

Thank you for being so kind and thoughtful

We are so grateful for the comfort you have provided in an
hour of need

Belonging to your wonderful congregation has been a
healing journey

You have always brought sunshine to those around you

FAMOUS QUOTES

Religion is to do right, it is to love,
it is to serve, it is to think,
it is to be humble.

—Ralph Waldo Emerson

All religions must be tolerated . . . for . . . every man
must get to heaven in his own way.

—Epictetus

Helpful Hints for How to Write a Toast

$\mathcal{Y}$ou have been given the honor of making the wedding toast. Stop hyperventilating! It is not that difficult to give a meaningful toast, even if you dislike public speaking. After all, these are people you know and love.

No matter what the occasion, whether it's a wedding, special birthday, or retirement, the basics in preparing a toast are the same.

One of the best ways to start a toast is with a short personal story. A story will serve as a showcase for the endearing traits you wish to highlight about the honoree. Is the person being toasted known for having a great sense of humor? A fabulous head of red hair? Two left feet? Tell the story of that fishing trip, or that kitchen redecorating fiasco, or that surprise birthday party, in which your best friend's wacky sense of humor, or your mother's enviable red hair, or your business colleague's klutziness, played a significant part. Not only will the story draw your audience in, it will touch the heart of the person being toasted.

Once you have the story you wish to tell in mind, write down a few notes, the outline of the story; never write your toast out word for word The last thing you want to do is stand in front of a group with your eyes glued to a piece of paper as you read aloud—you will look and sound mechanical. You want to appear spontaneous (even if you have practiced giving the toast a zillion times) and speak in a warm, conversational tone. So what you'll want is some three-by-five note cards with just the outline of key words, names, dates, and phrases that you can glance at now and then to prompt yourself as you speak.

Close your short opening story about the honoree by listing those characteristics that make this person so special to you and all of his friends, coworkers, and family. For instance, thank the honoree for his or her warmth, sense of humor, generosity, loyalty, and kindness. This will then take you to the toast itself; raise your glass and, on behalf of yourself and everyone gathered, wish your brother/mother/best friend more years of good health, wealth, and joy. Use any of the phrases and/or famous quotations in this book for the toast itself.

Above all: be sincere, have fun, and keep it short—anywhere from five to fifteen minutes. Brevity is the soul of wit!

Toasts

BIRTH

To ____, who will eternally be a symbol of your love

To the happy couple and their special gift from God

There is nothing as glorious as hearing a baby's laughter first
thing in the morning. Congratulations on the birth of your
new baby

To ____, who is the true expression of God's love

To ____, who will always be Daddy's little girl/boy and
Mommy's little angel

Enjoy every single day with your new baby, as time slips by so fast!

Congratulations on the birth of your new baby. The happy times are only beginning!

With the birth of your beautiful baby boy/girl, may your life be full of much happiness and many blessings

May your heart overflow with love and joy with the birth of your beautiful baby boy/girl

To ____, who will make life complete for Mommy and Daddy

To ____ and ____, may the angels smile down upon your beautiful new baby

To ____, may love, happiness, and laughter abide with you and your parents always

To ____ and ____, the waiting is finally over! Congratulations!

God bless you and God bless ____ on this wonderful day

There is nothing as joyous as the laughter of a baby in your home

To ____, and the wonderful parents that he/she chose

Congratulations on the birth of your new baby! Does he/she
  come with a book of instructions?
Congratulations to the new parents on the birth of one of
  life's most precious treasures
Congratulations and welcome to the new world of changing
  diapers, two-AM feedings, and very little sleep! You'll love it!

WEDDING

To ___ and ___, may the sun always shine on this glorious union

Well, it's too late for either of you to back out now! Wishing you both a lifetime of love and happiness

Cupid shot his arrow, and thank heavens neither of you ducked

May this wonderful day be an inspiration to you both for the rest of your lives

Congratulations to a wonderful couple as you celebrate a very special love

All the best always to the happy couple. To know them is to love them.

May your marriage sparkle like raindrops in the morning sun

To ____ and ____, may your wedding rings be a continuous reminder of the special love you share

To ____ and ____, from this day forward may your hearts forever be entwined

Wishing two of the greatest people in the world decades of love and happiness

May the joy you share today multiply tenfold through the years

To the happy couple, on the first day of the rest of their life together

May God bless this wonderful union forever

May your marriage be filled with health, wealth, and a great sense of humor

May the circle of your wedding bands remind you of your never-ending love

Wishing two soul mates and best friends a lifetime of love and dreams come true

Congratulations to two people who were always meant for each other

Wishing a perfect couple a perfect life
May the glow of love continue to grow throughout your
lifetime together
May the angels watch over you as you walk the path of
wedded bliss

RETIREMENT

$\mathcal{T}$o ____, may your retirement be the beginning of your happiest years

From today on, may all your wishes and dreams come true

May all your days be full of happiness, joy, and laughter

It's finally time for that great vacation you've planned, and you don't have to go to work on Monday!

You've worked so hard and the day is finally here! Happy retirement!

Wherever you go and whatever you do, may the sunshine always follow you

You can finally have fun, do what you feel like doing, and sleep till noon!

May you and your family enjoy all the happiness of your retirement years

All your years of hard work have finally paid off! Happy retirement!

It's time for sunshine, umbrella drinks, and swaying palm trees! Enjoy!

Here's to your retirement. Though I hear that due to the price of gas, your retirement home will be built in your backyard!

Your faithful friends have all gathered here to wish you a very happy retirement

Don't think of it as retirement, think of it as the beginning of a long voyage to *old age*!

We are here to commemorate this special day as you begin your well-deserved retirement

Though you didn't want a retirement celebration, you knew you could depend on us not to listen to you!

You finally have time to pamper yourself

Hold your glasses high, and always remember "the good old days"!

Now it's time to step away from the computer and pick up
the fishing pole!
You will be forever in our hearts and minds. Congratulations
and happy retirement!
Wishing you a lifetime full of great adventures!

BIRTHDAY

*Y*ou have brightened our days so often, and now it's our turn to brighten yours. Happy birthday!

Wishing you health, wealth, and happiness on your special day

You have made so many friends and we are all so pleased to be able to celebrate this special birthday with you

Celebrating a birthday isn't so bad, when you consider the alternative! Happy birthday!

Being "over the hill" isn't so bad. It's better than being under it!

May you always keep this birthday celebration as a fond memory. It is a sincere tribute from true friends.

May this birthday be as unforgettable as you

May you always have sweet memories of your ____ birthday celebration

Wishing you a lifetime full of sunny days and much love and laughter

How blessed we are to have a friend as true as you. Happy birthday!

Happy ____ birthday! Don't worry, it's only a number. A very *large* number!

May this birthday be the beginning of a year when all your wishes come true

Wishing a very special person a very special birthday

Happy birthday to someone who looks fairly good for his/her age!

As we gather together to celebrate your ____ birthday, let us raise our glasses to toast one super birthday guy/gal

May this birthday be one of your most outstanding memories

We are all so pleased to be here to help celebrate your birthday. Wishing you a very happy birthday and many, many more.

May this wonderful birthday party be an expression of our
deep affection for you. To the best! Happy birthday!
May this birthday be one of your most unforgettable ones!
You have been an inspiration to all of us and it gives us great
pleasure to be able to wish you a very happy birthday!

ANNIVERSARY

I have never met two people more compatible.
   Congratulations on your ____ anniversary!

May the love you share grow stronger with each passing year

I can't believe you've been married for ____ years. You still
   act like newlyweds!

Wishing you both every happiness as you celebrate the love
   you share

How could you two put up with each other for all these
   years? It must be love.

It is so wonderful to be able to share this day with two of my
   favorite people. Many blessings and happy anniversary.

It is difficult to be perfect, but you two do it with such ease.
   Congratulations and best wishes.

You two are a shining example of what love and happiness
    should be

You have shown us all what it's like to be happily married
    for ____ years. Congratulations!

Your love and devotion have been an inspiration to us all.
    May you share many more years of happiness together.

May the angels watch over you always, and especially today
    as you celebrate your ____ anniversary

We are so pleased to be able to share this wonderful
    celebration of your devotion to each other.
    Congratulations!

It takes the patience of a saint to be married as long as you
    two have. Happiness always!

Wishing two people who have always been there for each
    other all the happiness they so richly deserve

As we toast two of the happiest people we know, we hope it
    touches your hearts as much as you have touched ours

Wishing you much love, laughter, and happiness, now and
    forever

The magic of your love is contagious. Congratulations!

Your continuous love and devotion have been a perfect
example of what true love should be

We hope that all the joy of this wonderful occasion will
always be there to warm your hearts

We are so happy to be here to help two special people
celebrate their very special love

AWARD CEREMONY

You have proven that a goal is never out of reach if you
    work hard and have faith in yourself

You took on the difficult challenge and were successful!
    Congratulations!

I just cannot believe you got this award without my help!
    Way to go!

Congratulations on receiving this impressive award. You are
    on your way to a brilliant future.

Your exceptional work has led you to this well-deserved
    award

We are all united in wishing you many congratulations on
    receiving this very important award

We are all so proud of your accomplishment. Please know
that our good wishes will always be with you.

Now that you have won this outstanding award, the sky's the
limit!

As we observe this wonderful celebration of your
accomplishment, let us raise our glasses as an expression of
our heartiest congratulations

We're so proud of you for a job well done

Congratulations and best wishes. Your complete dedication
has earned you this wonderful award.

What a great honor this is, and no one deserves it more

Congratulations on being the winner we always knew you
were

With this award, a whole new world will open up for you

Congratulations on reaching the goal you have strived so
hard to attain

What a tremendous honor it is to receive this award.
Congratulations and best wishes always.

With the winning of this award, you are an inspiration to all
of us. Congratulations.

I would like to commend you on winning this prestigious
award

Winning this award is just the beginning of many wonderful
things

FRIENDSHIP

*T*o a friend who has been a gift from God, may the angels
watch over you always

Sending heartfelt words of thanks to a true friend whose
tireless devotion has meant so much to us

To you, my friend, whose kindness and thoughtfulness have
always made you the special person you are

As we gather together to celebrate this special day, let us toast
our dear friend with many wishes for a future full of
happiness and joy

We have had so many happy moments to remember, and this
day is now one of them

Your friendship has always been something that I have
treasured

True friends share a special bond that lasts a lifetime

We can't choose our relatives, but thank goodness we can
   choose our friends, and I'm so glad I chose you

It warms my heart to remember all the many happy times we
   have shared

I consider your friendship to be the most precious gift I possess

To an old friend I just met!

To a lifelong friend who has made my life more beautiful

We have been friends since we were kids. Thank you for
   always being there for me.

Life is a patchwork of friends, and you are the center star

Through the years no one has known me better than you, my
   dear friend

To my friend, who has filled my life with laughter and sunshine

To you, my best friend, many thanks for all our happy
   memories

Neither time nor distance can separate true friends

Don't ever move away, my friend. You know too much!

Our friendship has meant so much to me through all these
   years

BRIDAL SHOWER

*M*ay this happy day be pressed in your book of memories
   as one of your most precious moments

May the magic of your love last forever and ever

The most important thing for a bride-to-be to remember is
   to always keep your sense of humor nearby

Let us raise our glasses in celebration of this very special love

Wishing you and ____ a lifetime full of love, laughter, and
   happiness

May the glow of love and happiness in your eyes today light
   up your heart forever

Your exceptional love is a wonderful example to all of us.
   Congratulations.

To you and ____: you are the perfect couple, and we are all so
   happy about your forthcoming marriage

May this be the beginning of turning many happy moments into joyful memories

Remember, when you have walked down the aisle and the priest/preacher/rabbi says, "Do you take this man," the response is "I do," not "Whatever!"

Wishing the bride-to-be all the love and happiness her heart can hold

Well, you finally hooked him! Congratulations and best wishes always.

Love makes life sweeter. Happiness always to the bride-to-be.

You've searched the world over and finally found your heart's desire

May this be the beginning of many magical moments in your future

May the angels be with you as you head down the path to wedded bliss

As you walk hand in hand and heart to heart, may all your dreams come true

May your wedded life be as special as you are

Wishing you a lifetime full of joy, health, and prosperity

As we gather for this wonderful occasion, let us lift our
   glasses and wish the bride-to-be and the love of her life
   all the happiness they so richly deserve

ENGAGEMENT

*M*ay you always look at each other as you do today, with
   such love and devotion

May the romance you share always be with you

To the happy couple . . . wishing you both a life full of wishes
   come true

As you walk hand in hand through life, may the angels always
   watch over you

Always remember to hold both her hands tightly (so she can't
   get to the credit cards!)

Wishing God's blessings to two dear friends as you begin
   your journey to join two hearts into one

Sending many happy wishes to the future bride and groom
   for much happiness and good fortune

As we gather together today to celebrate this most happy

occasion, I predict a long and happy life for two of the dearest people I know

True love means patience, understanding, compassion, compromise, and a really great sense of humor! You have shown you have it all!

May your love blossom as you travel down the road to wedded bliss

There are two phrases that the happy couple should always keep on the tip of their tongues:

    Bride-to-be: "Honey, would you please . . ."

    Groom-to-be: "Yes, dear."

As you start down the path to wedded joy, may you both find happiness at the end of the rainbow

May all the love you have found continue to grow endlessly

Wishing two great people all the love and happiness their hearts can hold

This is the beginning of the sweet journey to the day when you say "I do"

You've finally made it official and you can't back out of it!

Your love is a special gift to share for the rest of your lives

Now that you're starting out on the happiest journey of your life, make certain to keep your sense of humor!

Wishing you both a life full of love and laughter

All of us join in to wish the happy couple a perfect day and a perfect life

GRADUATION

You finally graduated! We're so proud, but why does your diploma say "Toy Store"?

Now that you have graduated, I predict an excellent career because of your remarkable abilities. Congratulations, graduate!

As we gather together to share in this auspicious occasion, we would like to toast the graduate with many congratulations

Because of your diligence and hard work, you have been a source of great pride to the family. Congratulations!

May your future flourish now that you have graduated

We are all pleased to be here to pay tribute to a wonderful person who has proved to be an exceptional graduate. The best of everything to you always.

We have all patiently waited for this happy day to come. Congratulations.

Congratulations on your graduation. You now have a successful and prosperous future to look forward to.

There is no time more fitting than now to wish you an incredible future and much success

You have set the perfect example for anyone to follow. Your diligence and dedication have made you the successful person you are today. Congratulations.

All your hard work and dedication has finally paid off. Congratulations on your graduation.

You have reached for the stars with much patience and diligence, and they are now yours

You have finally graduated and it was without my help! However did that happen?

Congratulations, graduate. Your brilliant future has now begun.

Because of all your hard work, there is nothing but success in your future

May all you have strived for be yours for the taking now

Now that you have graduated, may all your visions for the
future be happy and bright

You have made us all so proud of your accomplishments.
Congratulations!

To you and your outstanding record of accomplishments!
Way to go!

Your dedication has been an inspiration to us all.
Congratulations, graduate!

MOM/DAD/PARENTS

$\mathscr{A}$ddress the following phrases to your mother, father, or both your parents:

We are so blessed to have you as our mother

Here's to you, Dad. You have not only been my father, but also my best friend

To Mom . . . you are more special than any words could ever say

Mom and Dad, we hope that this celebration begins to show you how grateful we are for all the years of your loving and caring

To Mom, whose loving arms have always been a safe haven from all our problems

To Mom, who can attribute every gray hair she has to me!

We have so many happy memories of the parties and celebrations you had for us. We hope we have shown how grateful we are by giving you this special celebration of your own.

May the angels always watch over you, as you have always watched over us

Today is your day, Mom! We are so happy to give back today a small part of all the love you have given us through the years.

Dad, you have sacrificed so much for us, and we hope today is the day we can make your wishes and dreams come true

You have touched our lives in so many wonderful ways, Mom. Thank you for always being there for us.

To Mom, who has the love of an angel and the patience of a saint!

Mom and Dad, now that I am a mother/father, I can finally understand and appreciate everything you went through

Dad, you have always been there for us, and we'd just like to let you know that we are always here for you

There is nothing that gives me more joy than to let you know how important you are to me

Your unconditional love and guidance have made me the caring person I am today. Thank you.

No one envies the job a mother does. She wears many hats, works long hours, and is underpaid. But Mom, you are the example I will always carry in my heart.

I have been so fortunate to have you as my father. I treasure each moment of shared memories.

To Dad, thank you for your warm and caring heart, and all the love and laughter you keep in our home

Though I don't say it often enough, thank you for being my parents!

HOUSEWARMING

*M*ay your new home be filled with peace, love, and
harmony

May your home always be a refuge from the hectic world
outside

It's so great to own your own home. No more asking
permission to hang a picture!

From now on you will have all the joys of home ownership:
lawn care, mortgage payments, snow blowing, leaf raking,
and plumbing problems!

Now that you have a home of your own, you will find out
that there really is no place like home!

There's an old saying that says, "New home, new baby."
Best wishes for both!

May God forever bless the people who dwell in this
wonderful home

The love you share will always make your house a home

The charm and elegance of your new home makes visitors
feel completely comfortable

May the angels live within these walls and watch over all who
dwell within

Wishing you many heartfelt congratulations as you become a
homeowner

A house full of laughter and love soon becomes a real home,
and you have a great start

As you begin your life in your new home, you are beginning
a lifetime of happy memories

We are bringing a bouquet of good wishes as you open the
door of your new home to family and friends

May your new home always overflow with love and
happiness

As we celebrate this wonderful occasion, we know that all
your dreams and wishes have finally come true

Wishing you and your family all the happiness your hearts
can hold as you enjoy your home

We all join in wishing you peace and joy in your new home

Wishing you many blessings as you celebrate all four seasons
in your new home

Live life to the fullest, enjoy your new home, and keep in
mind that dust is a country accent!

DIVORCE PARTY

*W*ho would have thought that losing 180 pounds would be so easy! Congratulations!

It's about time you can finally start living your life. Have a ball!

We are so proud of you. Congratulations on being a survivor!

Today is the day you begin building a brand-new life

Put one foot in front of the other to begin your new journey in really living

You have finally cut the cord and life can be beautiful once again

Breaking free can be quite an exciting adventure!

It's a great time to look back and say, "Thank heavens he's finally gone!"

Isn't it great to finally be able to get on with your own life?
Congratulations.

You will discover that a divorce is a very healing journey to a
greater life

With all our love and encouragement, you are now able to go
on to bigger and better things

We have gathered together here to show our support for this
major decision. Way to go!

Please know that you are surrounded by friendship as you
begin to enjoy your well-deserved freedom

Start making a list of all the new experiences you are now free
to discover. Happy divorce!

You will now realize it is such a relief not to have to answer to
anyone. Enjoy!

You now have the power to embrace your new life and fulfill
all your dreams

Happy divorce! Now don't forget to get rid of the voodoo
doll!

This is now the perfect time to reclaim your life. Make every
    day count.
Don't be discouraged. Prince Charming is still out there!
Now that you are divorced, there's a whole new wonderful
    life out there waiting to be lived

GOOD-BYE PARTY

𝐼t is so difficult to say good-bye, but keep in mind we will
   always be with you in spirit

As you depart, you take with you all our good wishes for
   health, happiness, and prosperity

We all hate to see you leave, but we are so proud of you for
   taking on this new venture

As we bid you a fond farewell, please know you are taking all
   our good wishes and admiration with you

We're really going to miss you. By the way, the movers will be
   there this afternoon!

Let us not say good-bye, let us just say, "Till we meet again"

We are really going to miss your generous smile, great sense
   of humor, and your caring personality

Though it is time to say good-bye to you, we wish you much happiness in your brilliant new future

It is very difficult to say good-bye, but please know that the example you have set will always be remembered

Good-bye, good luck, and don't slack off at your new job!

May God bless you on this journey into a new and exciting life

As we toast your departure, please know you are taking with you our warmest personal regards

Best wishes for the wonderful life you so richly deserve

You have worked so hard to achieve this goal. Way to go!

We have come together for this grand celebration to show you how much we respect and admire you. You will be missed.

Godspeed as you begin your interesting and exciting new journey

We have so many happy memories, I find it difficult to say good-bye

As we are all gathered together here to say good-bye, we
  predict that all your goals will be reached
As we come together for this farewell party, we join in
  wishing you Godspeed as you begin your exciting new life
It is with much sadness that we are faced with having to say
  good-bye to a very special person

BABY SHOWER

*T*here is nothing that brings so much joy as bringing a new
   life into the family

Showering many of God's blessings upon you and your
   baby-to-be

Wishing you all possible joy and happiness as you await the
   birth of your baby

Many heartfelt congratulations on the upcoming birth of
   your bundle of joy

You think the difficult part is the delivery. Oh no, it's the
   two-AM feedings and the dirty diapers!

Babies don't come with a book of instructions. It's a learn-as-
   you-go process. Congratulations!

You look so beautiful as you are on your way to parenthood.
   May the angels watch over you always.

May your new baby bring you happiness and joy forever

May the angels bless and watch over you and your family as you await the coming of your new baby

A baby is a wonderful blessing from above. But remember to keep your sense of humor—you'll need it!

There is nothing as sweet as the scent of a baby nuzzling on your shoulder

With the birth of your baby, you are in for much joy, laughter, and fun

Your new baby will touch your heart forever

Enjoy every single moment with your new baby, since they grow up so fast—they're in school before you know it!

May your new baby be a ray of sunshine to you and your loved ones

With the upcoming birth of your new baby, you are on the way to all your dreams coming true

May your holidays be more precious as you await the birth of your bundle of joy

Your baby's birth will be an eternal symbol of your love

As we gather to celebrate the impending birth of your baby, let us raise our glasses to wish you and your family all the joy and happiness you deserve

Today is the day we celebrate a very special love. There is no bond as strong as the one between mother and child. Blessings always.

International Toasts

A votre santé! (France)
Cheers! (Britain)
Na zdrowie! (Poland)
Ooogy wawa! (Africa—Zulu)
Prosit! (Germany)
Salud! (Spain)
Skål! (Sweden)
Sláinte! (Ireland)
Wen lie! (China)
Yamas! (Greece)
Salute! (Italy)
Za vashe zdorovie! (Russia)

State Abbreviations

Alabama—AL

Alaska—AK

Arizona—AZ

Arkansas—AR

California—CA

Colorado—CO

Connecticut—CT

Delaware—DE

District of Columbia—DC

Florida—FL

Georgia—GA

Hawaii—HI

Idaho—ID

Illinois—IL

Indiana—IN

Iowa—IA

Kansas—KS

Kentucky—KY

Louisiana—LA

Maine—ME

Maryland—MD

Massachusetts—MA

Michigan—MI

Minnesota—MN

Mississippi—MS

Missouri—MO

Montana—MT

Nebraska—NE

Nevada—NV

New Hampshire—NH

New Jersey—NJ

New Mexico—NM

New York—NY

North Carolina—NC

North Dakota—ND

Ohio—OH

Oklahoma—OK

Oregon—OR

Pennsylvania—PA

Rhode Island—RI

South Carolina—SC

South Dakota—SD

Tennessee—TN

Texas—TX

Utah—UT

Vermont—VT

Virginia—VA

Washington—WA

West Virginia—WV

Wisconsin—WI

Wyoming—WY

Card Recipient Lists

GRANDPARENTS DAY

Valentine's Day

St. Patrick's Day

_____

_____

_____

_____

_____

_____

_____

_____

Halloween

_____

_____

_____

_____

_____

_____

_____

_____

THANKSGIVING

_____

_____

_____

_____

_____

_____

_____

_____

NATIONAL BOSS DAY

_____

_____

_____

_____

_____

_____

_____

_____

NATIONAL NURSES DAY

_____

_____

_____

_____

_____

_____

_____

_____

Administrative Professionals (Secretaries) Day

NATIONAL TEACHER DAY

PHYSICIANS

_____

_____

_____

_____

_____

_____

_____

_____

ATTORNEYS

CLERGY

_____

_____

_____

_____

_____

_____

_____

_____